when voices

detach
themselves

when voices

detach
themselves

gary lundy

MISSOULA, MT & MINNEAPOLIS, MN

Poetry

Cover art: *A Falling into Light* ©2013 Ian Mahon
Faceplate: *How Deep the Cut that Bleeds* ©2013 Ian Mahon

is a rose press publishes poetry, poetics, experimental writing, cross-genre and other work. We are a cooperative editorial board of writers in the virtual world. Submissions are by invitation only at this time. Check our website for updates and changes in this policy.

Website: isarosepress.WordPress.com

lundy, gary
      when voices detach themselves

      is a rose press
      1. Poetry. 2. LGBT poetry. 3.Love poetry. I. Title: when voices detach themselves.

ISBN 978-0-9896245-0-3

for my friends

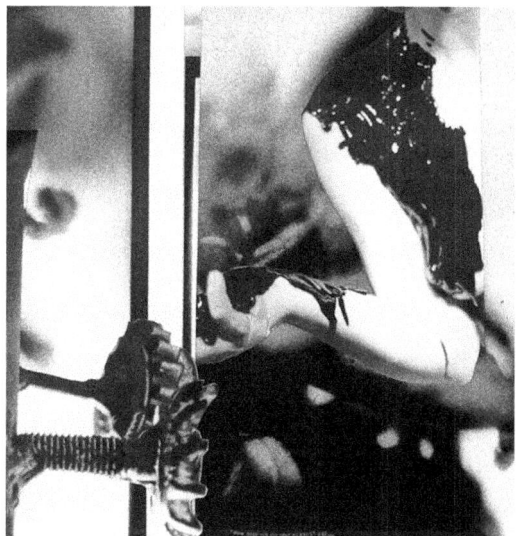

when voices detach themselves. when i imagine i am listening to their speakers sudden impact of invisibility. of having lost the way. even though insistence attempts to sidestep a bouncing young noise. can it be. that through thought i confirm my being. yet does it too proceed the thought. can it not outlast loss.

in another location two people unwind their bodies from the previous nights encounter. move to opposite sides of the room.

hope to be prepared. to experience that fluid moment ripe in its promise of pleasure. to move becomes its own motivator. a song unlike top forty love song. yet deeply involved in love. to be within the unrestricted space moments before the eighteen wheeler rolls onto your side of the highway blocking escape. those awkward flashes prior to the grip of fear. water beats the flower garden into muddy collection of color shards. she will no longer speak to you. he washes his hands in the deep sink.

direction remains a curiosity as i stand outside the front door smoking. finishing a dull butt of tobacco. as if driven by intuition i face the northwest. seek some kind of miracle. like a kindness recognized. as *love*. yet my mind tricks me into believing i face the east. the certainty of my lover whose body pulsates. moves closer to the canvas. then suddenly back near the palate of colors. clean and clear. smoky in surprise. i snuff the bud and reenter my home. hold still to my lover and to the promise of the other who may one day become new lover. vicinity as proximity. align both in the compass hair of projections.

he wants to believe in kindness. but cannot. not in this life. where belief suffers the constant constraint of fear. then attacks. where his family evaporates. his friends. the sound of distance silence elongates. there's a moment when giving up solves. the solution. there can be little joy unattached from need. no pleasure unattached from wants. demands.

there are always gaps even in the most secure and pristine narratives where all the real action takes place. the field of the arbitrary.

i have been one to believe in perfection. in my imagination my lover never smells of hard work or simple day. relationships last forever. are thus something to give ones life to. last night as i pulled the sheet and summer quilt over my shoulders to kiss my face i smelled my father and knew finally that he was indeed real. just now i followed a wisp of smoke back into my house.

i should want to call my lover. to hear his beautiful voice and laughter. but i don't. even when i think about it. perhaps because it's easiest to keep him fresh and alive in memory as he was before i left. frequently in the night i am awakened by his footsteps quietly approaching. phantom pain. he remains thousands of miles away. hours impossible to gauge. for so long now the distance resembles a third lover. cruel and possessive. repressive like a hard thunderstorm. rain heavy and powerful. we sit alone. neither able to call. repeat under our tongues a quiet *my love*.

he wonders if others see the mask of approaching death on his face. he's read that this is possible. wonders whether he's simply lived a charmed life since he's never noticed this on any of the faces he's seen. but would he know what he's looking for. that fact haunts as he washes his face and stares into the mirror. seeing little he recognizes.

when my father died. the night before he visited my dreams. all night. until i finally told him it was all right to go. that we were all able to care for ourselves.

my brother says he awoke to see our father standing at the foot of his bed. he knew then our father had died.

looking for reentrance into my writing
again i find this.

i'm allergic to the man i love.
a common enough affliction known as distance.

your flattery will get you into my pants to be sure.

the writing itself affirms.

as i have to do i bring this to a more personal level. certainly in my writing part of the task has been to find a form that not only expresses what i have lived. but the stories of what i can live. feel certain that every marginalized person has this task. or remains subordinate and enslaved. yet as i struggle with the how of actualizing this. or getting to the story not in unremarkable and familiar narrative. i realize how troubling and difficult it is.

i apologize for loading you down with images. just excited to get closer to present. and maybe a future.

i am used to waiting. he believes it turns into science. she scavenges among glaciers attempting one brief flight of vision. a bicycle cranks outside in the breeze. looking at my left arm i wonder if tattoos like hair keep heat in. ferocity may be either inherent or learned.

intimacy pretends a possibility of knowing another inside and out without the obscuring principle of thought.

when you strip before the camera. anonymity impresses the skin. try to push back. impose gravity. like music in a cafe. settle amidst dust. impose on electrical outlet. he flatters himself. says repetitively. *you're beautiful*. meaning really. *i love proximity*.

ten minutes now fence the field.

put a line back in.

right now i have my mouth on your beautiful skin.
my hands on your cock. i am loving you with skin.
tongue. being into and with your being. it's slow.
not methodical. but precise. i take you entire into
my mouth. my throat. to languish and fluidly
swallow. i hold you. you may cry. do. let your fear
out. you are safe. *i love you*.

what i need is the sense of beginning. an excitement. confusion. even the contingency built into activity that is new.

life is majority of time contingent. we build all sorts of external and internal constructs to ward off that fact. the accidental nature makes use of the contingent rather than thought upon thought upon thought that finally elopes into the world as if new and fresh. when simple regurgitation.

he will be unable to take his desire into her world without giving up the possibility of control. to stand where her eyes take him in and accept or reject as if he were merely another one of her poems. no effort at compliment will protect him. his words finally signify nothing. abscessing silence.

from that place patriarchy attempts to erase
a nonlinear site.

gary lundy

you read buttons. he scribbles onto a page
deliberate hope.
solitude over the icelandic phone call leaning
toward a vacuous booth.

pre-ordained.

what it means to be. in any language. a man. but
to swear off men. for the summer. means to be
elsewhere than in familiar. to lapse into an older
memory. one that dreams into a belonging.
longing toward the mother. lapsing toward a
deliberate forgetting. where cocks congregate
voicing displeasure. remember nature. how the
small bird. in the other bedroom flies against
pains and glass. she wears your shirt and you
suddenly feel what it means to be captive. of
beauty. erosion.

15

episodic *i*. to begin believing in solitary rawness in *i* over displaced *you*. *her*. or *him*. to believe. as if. the *i* closer to truth. a present fact of having been here at least this once. to begin. the sentence with the article *a*. no being present. a photograph of one of your lovers left breast veiled through lace nipple relaxed arm lifted to reveal hairless.

shine the light onto the prosaic room. unsettle the assortment of you having lived there. still breathing. wonder into the collage portrait of one of those whom you love. who remains absent. voices muffle into droplets collecting in corners of the other room. the dark one. flamboyant in displacement. place the cup onto the saucer upon the table top. listen to background music. a mother and two children. soft suddenly yesterday. episode.

august. in early june. night rain. moisture sponge.
chill breeze. he elopes into dream. of having you.
the want palpable. as coffee and scone drowns
the morning web. mind another business. outside
any sort of salvation. *come save me*. he thinks.
looks toward the northwest. this time. before.
a light pause between the albums fourth and
fifth tracks. advance today back into the bright
morning darkness. cloud cover and soft shadows.
flamboyant prosaic.

elemental parataxis. disguise desire beneath a black t. wear the blue smile of rising out into memory. no one is who they were supposed to be. all grown up. remarkable beauty mark. she smiles and listens aloud in the broad sunlight. last nights rain. i can always be crazy like that. between two potential lovers. give it all seven miles down the road. a kindred to loving your mother. wood squeaks. old bar stools complain. there can be a kind of remembering that flows out of tomorrow. this afternoon.

a fear of losing what has already been purchased over time in correspondence keeps his heart alive with anticipation nearly overwhelming practical facts as distance and gender. he would give up men. he thinks. at least for the summer. if it gives permission to their reading of bodies conjoined. such promise of melodic prose. yet he remains scarred enough to know that improbability holds greater likelihood. a promise in the wind of evening rain.

fight against the page its restrictions desire to spread delicate wings of uncommon words past the edge that they might fly like love permeating this usual story.

being unable to hear
the answer
he fails even to construct
a question

words are photographs and i follow their lead as if following you your eyes or thoughts all the time knowing with implicit blue lips that nothing has evidently changed even though you see three bighorn sheep out your front window and i look onto your anonymous body legs leaning away camera face wondering how i might have felt so happy and sad simultaneously.

she wonders at his incessant talk. as if. to keep at bay some night time panic. like two women talking their faith to each other. as if. it was real. she rests in listening. turns over in her mind why she ever chose to visit. what about him appeals through their distant correspondence. she stumbles. realizes he's waiting her voice. yet still caught in the rapid page turning of her desire she says. *are you hungry*. laughs at such an inappropriate exclusion.

he realizes what he yearns for is to be loved. common malady. what he felt when you were there. in his home. yet how to have love without complicating it with desire. to imagine always *the more*.

i love you. am in love with you. desire your body and soul. he thinks out loud.

he knew that
he just didn't trust
the timing
what he knew
to say
so said it wrong

as out of remarkable past
a slight look aside peripheral desire
another over written story lies
indeed it may only be overdue bills
envelopes stacked against the south wall
last years dishes among the growing mold

you came to me later after other women had taught me their possibility and mine while men kept warning their usual mantra it is a mans world but it isn't after all and a reality exists outside even their peripheral gaze even outside their understanding a desire full of exception and expectation for a different kind of language a different kind of life where ego shrinks to the size of a pea and life becomes quite suddenly more about more than usual

upon the pockmarked body of my lovers dark skin
i lay to rest all my love being incapable of more i
mouth the *i love you* around and upon his lovely
cock until its focus consumes my mouth.

gary lundy

About the author

gary lundy is the author of three poetry chapbooks: *this making i tore the sight from*, *lavish is saying nothing like again*, and *to each other water cool and pure*. His work has appeared in a variety of magazines and journals including: *Spout*, *Main Street Rag*, *Taproot Literary Review*, *The Rockford Review*, *RiversEdge*, *Voices Israel*, *ditch*, *The Bicycle Review*, *Down in the Dirt*, *Askew*, *My Favorite Bullet*, *Cedilla*, and *Indefinite Space*. He lives in Missoula, Montana.